FOREWORD

The collection of "Everything Will Be Okay" travel phrasebooks published by T&P Books is designed for people traveling abroad for tourism and business. The phrasebooks contain what matters most - the essentials for basic communication. This is an indispensable set of phrases to "survive" while abroad.

This phrasebook will help you in most cases where you need to ask something, get directions, find out how much something costs, etc. It can also resolve difficult communication situations where gestures just won't help.

This book contains a lot of phrases that have been grouped according to the most relevant topics. You'll also find a mini dictionary with useful words - numbers, time, calendar, colors...

Take "Everything Will Be Okay" phrasebook with you on the road and you'll have an irreplaceable traveling companion who will help you find your way out of any situation and teach you to not fear speaking with foreigners.

TABLE OF CONTENTS

T&P Books Publishing

T&P Books Publishing

PHRASEBOOK

— UZBEK —

THE MOST IMPORTANT PHRASES

This phrasebook contains
the most important
phrases and questions
for basic communication
Everything you need
to survive overseas

By Andrey Taranov

T&P BOOKS

Phrasebook + 250-word dictionary

English-Uzbek phrasebook & mini dictionary

By Andrey Taranov

The collection of "Everything Will Be Okay" travel phrasebooks published by T&P Books is designed for people traveling abroad for tourism and business. The phrasebooks contain what matters most - the essentials for basic communication. This is an indispensable set of phrases to "survive" while abroad.

You'll also find a mini dictionary with 250 useful words required for everyday communication - the names of months and days of the week, measurements, family members, and more.

T&P Books Publishing
www.tpbooks.com

ISBN: 978-1-80001-566-1

This book is also available in E-book formats.
Please visit www.tpbooks.com or the major online bookstores.

PRONUNCIATION

Letter	Uzbek example	T&P phonetic alphabet	English example
A a	satr	[a]	shorter than in ask
B b	kutubxona	[b]	baby, book
D d	marvarid	[d]	day, doctor
E e	erkin	[e]	elm, medal
F f	mukofot	[f]	face, food
G g	girdob	[g]	game, gold
G' g'	g'ildirak	[ɣ]	between [g] and [h]
H h	hasharot	[h]	home, have
I i	kirish	[i], [iː]	feet, Peter
J j	natija	[dʒ]	joke, general
K k	namlik	[k]	clock, kiss
L l	talaffuz	[l]	lace, people
M m	tarjima	[m]	magic, milk
N n	nusxa	[n]	name, normal
O o	bosim	[ɒ], [o]	bottle, clock
O' o'	o'simlik	[ø]	eternal, church
P p	polapon	[p]	pencil, private
Q q	qor	[q]	king, club
R r	rozilik	[r]	rice, radio
S s	siz	[s]	city, boss
T t	tashkilot	[t]	tourist, trip
U u	uchuvchi	[u]	book
V v	vergul	[w]	vase, winter
X x	xonadon	[ħ]	humor
Y y	yigit	[j]	yes, New York
Z z	zirak	[z]	zebra, please
ch	chang	[tʃ]	church, French
sh	shikoyat	[ʃ]	machine, shark
' '	san'at	[ː], [‒]	no sound

Comments

[1] [:] - Lengthens the preceding vowel; after consonants is used as a 'hard sign'

LIST OF ABBREVIATIONS

English abbreviations

ab.	-	about
adj	-	adjective
adv	-	adverb
anim.	-	animate
as adj	-	attributive noun used as adjective
e.g.	-	for example
etc.	-	et cetera
fam.	-	familiar
fem.	-	feminine
form.	-	formal
inanim.	-	inanimate
masc.	-	masculine
math	-	mathematics
mil.	-	military
n	-	noun
pl	-	plural
pron.	-	pronoun
sb	-	somebody
sing.	-	singular
sth	-	something
v aux	-	auxiliary verb
vi	-	intransitive verb
vi, vt	-	intransitive, transitive verb
vt	-	transitive verb

UZBEK
PHRASEBOOK

This section contains
important phrases that may
come in handy in various
real-life situations.
The phrasebook will help
you ask for directions, clarify
a price, buy tickets, and
order food at a restaurant

T&P Books Publishing

PHRASEBOOK CONTENTS

T&P Books Publishing

The bare minimum

Excuse me, ...

Кечирасиз, ...
Kechirasiz, ...

Hello.

Ассалому алайкум.
Assalomu alaykum.

Thank you.

Раҳмат.
Rahmat.

Good bye.

Кўришгунча.
Ko'rishguncha.

Yes.

Ҳа.
Ha.

No.

Йўқ.
Yo'q.

I don't know.

Билмайман.
Bilmayman.

Where? | Where to? | When?

Қаерда? | Қаерга? | Қачон?
Qaerda? | Qaerga? | Qachon?

I need ...

Менга ... керак.
Menga ... kerak.

I want ...

Мен ... хоҳлайман.
Men ... xohlayman.

Do you have ...?

Сизда ... борми?
Sizda ... bormi?

Is there a ... here?

Бу ерда ... борми?
Bu erda ... bormi?

May I ...?

Мен ... бўладими?
Men ... bo'ladimi?

..., please (polite request)

Марҳамат қилиб
Marhamat qilib

I'm looking for ...

Мен ... қидираяпман.
Men ... qidirayapman.

the restroom

ҳожатхона
hojatxona

an ATM

банкомат
bankomat

a pharmacy (drugstore)

дорихона
dorixona

a hospital

шифохона
shifoxona

the police station

милиция бўлимини
militsiya bo'limini

the subway

метро
metro

a taxi	**такси** taksi
the train station	**вокзал** vokzal

My name is ...	**Менинг исмим ...** Mening ismim ...
What's your name?	**Исмингиз нима?** Ismingiz nima?
Could you please help me?	**Менга ёрдам бериб юборинг,** **илтимос.** Menga yordam berib yuboring, iltimos.
I've got a problem.	**Менда бир муаммо бор.** Menda bir muammo bor.
I don't feel well.	**Аҳволим ёмон.** Ahvolim yomon.
Call an ambulance!	**Тез ёрдам чақиринг!** Tez yordam chaqiring!
May I make a call?	**Қўнғироқ қилсам бўладими?** Qo'ng'iroq qilsam bo'ladimi?

I'm sorry.	**Узр, ...** Uzr, ...
You're welcome.	**Арзимайди** Arzimaydi

I, me	**мен** men
you (inform.)	**сен** sen
he	**у** u
she	**у** u
they (masc.)	**улар** ular
they (fem.)	**улар** ular
we	**биз** biz
you (pl)	**сиз** siz
you (sg, form.)	**Сиз** Siz

ENTRANCE	**КИРИШ** KIRISH
EXIT	**ЧИҚИШ** CHIQISH
OUT OF ORDER	**ИШЛАМАЙДИ** ISHLAMAYDI

CLOSED	**ЁПИҚ** YOPIQ
OPEN	**ОЧИҚ** OCHIQ
FOR WOMEN	**АЁЛЛАР УЧУН** AYOLLAR UCHUN
FOR MEN	**ЭРКАКЛАР УЧУН** ERKAKLAR UCHUN

Questions

Where?	**Қаерда?** Qaerda?
Where to?	**Қаерга?** Qaerga?
Where from?	**Қаердан?** Qaerdan?
Why?	**Нимага?** Nimaga?
For what reason?	**Нима учун?** Nima uchun?
When?	**Қачон?** Qachon?
How long?	**Қанча вақт?** Qancha vaqt?
At what time?	**Нечада?** Nechada?
How much?	**Қанча туради?** Qancha turadi?
Do you have …?	**Сизда … борми?** Sizda … bormi?
Where is …?	**… қаерда жойлашган?** … qaerda joylashgan?
What time is it?	**Соат неча бўлди?** Soat necha bo'ldi?
May I make a call?	**Қўнғироқ қилсам бўладими?** Qo'ng'iroq qilsam bo'ladimi?
Who's there?	**Ким у?** Kim u?
Can I smoke here?	**Бу ерда чексам бўладими?** Bu erda cheksam bo'ladimi?
May I …?	**Мен … бўладими?** Men … bo'ladimi?

Needs

I'd like …	**Мен … истардим.** Men … istardim.
I don't want …	**Мен … истамайман.** Men … istamayman.
I'm thirsty.	**Мен ичишни хоҳлайман.** Men ichishni xohlayman.
I want to sleep.	**Мен ухлашни хоҳлайман.** Men uxlashni xohlayman.

I want …	**Мен … хоҳлайман.** Men … xohlayman.
to wash up	**ювинишни** yuvinishni
to brush my teeth	**тишларни тозалашни** tishlarni tozalashni
to rest a while	**бироз дам олишни** biroz dam olishni
to change my clothes	**кийимларимни алмаштиришни** kiyimlarimni almashtirishni

to go back to the hotel	**меҳмонхонага қайтиш** mehmonxonaga qaytish
to buy …	**… сотиб олиш** … sotib olish
to go to …	**…га бориб келиш** …ga borib kelish
to visit …	**… зиёрат қилиш** … ziyorat qilish
to meet with …	**… билан учрашиш** … bilan uchrashish
to make a call	**қўнғироқ қилиш** qo'ng'iroq qilish

I'm tired.	**Мен чарчадим.** Men charchadim.
We are tired.	**Биз чарчадик.** Biz charchadik.
I'm cold.	**Мен совқотдим.** Men sovqotdim.
I'm hot.	**Мен исиб кетдим.** Men isib ketdim.
I'm OK.	**Менга нормал.** Menga normal.

I need to make a call.	**Қўнғироқ қилишим керак.** Qo'ng'iroq qilishim kerak.
I need to go to the restroom.	**Ҳожатхонага боришим керак.** Hojatxonaga borishim kerak.
I have to go.	**Вақт бўлди.** Vaqt bo'ldi.
I have to go now.	**Боришим керак.** Borishim kerak.

Asking for directions

Excuse me, …	**Кечирасиз, …** Kechirasiz, …
Where is …?	**… қаерда жойлашган?** … qaerda joylashgan?
Which way is …?	**… қайси йўналишда жойлашган?** … qaysi yo'nalishda joylashgan?
Could you help me, please?	**Менга ёрдам бериб юборинг, илтимос.** Menga yordam berib yuboring, iltimos.

I'm looking for …	**Мен … қидираяпман.** Men … qidirayapman.
I'm looking for the exit.	**Мен чиқиш йўлини қидираяпман.** Men chiqish yo'lini qidirayapman.
I'm going to …	**Мен …га кетаяпман.** Men …ga ketayapman.
Am I going the right way to …?	**Мен …га тўғри кетаяпманми?** Men …ga to'g'ri ketayapmanmi?

Is it far?	**Бу узоқми?** Bu uzoqmi?
Can I get there on foot?	**У ерга пиёда бора оламанми?** U erga piyoda bora olamanmi?
Can you show me on the map?	**Илтимос, харитада кўрсатиб юборинг.** Iltimos, xaritada ko'rsatib yuboring.
Show me where we are right now.	**Ҳозир қаерда эканимизни кўрсатиб юборинг.** Hozir qaerda ekanimizni ko'rsatib yuboring.

Here	**Бу ерда** Bu erda
There	**У ерда** U erda
This way	**Бу томонга** Bu tomonga

Turn right.	**Ўнгга бурилинг.** O'ngga buriling.
Turn left.	**Чапга бурилинг.** Chapga buriling.

first (second, third) turn	**биринчи (иккинчи, учинчи) бурилиш** birinchi (ikkinchi, uchinchi) burilish
to the right	**ўнгга** o'ngga
to the left	**чапга** chapga
Go straight ahead.	**Тўғри боринг.** To'g'ri boring.

Signs

WELCOME!	**ХУШ КЕЛИБСИЗ!** XUSH KELIBSIZ!
ENTRANCE	**КИРИШ** KIRISH
EXIT	**ЧИҚИШ** CHIQISH
PUSH	**ЎЗИНГИЗДАН** O'ZINGIZDAN
PULL	**ЎЗИНГИЗГА** O'ZINGIZGA
OPEN	**ОЧИҚ** OCHIQ
CLOSED	**ЁПИҚ** YOPIQ
FOR WOMEN	**АЁЛЛАР УЧУН** AYOLLAR UCHUN
FOR MEN	**ЭРКАКЛАР УЧУН** ERKAKLAR UCHUN
GENTLEMEN, GENTS	**ЭРКАКЛАР ҲОЖАТХОНАСИ** ERKAKLAR HOJATXONASI
WOMEN	**АЁЛЛАР ҲОЖАТХОНАСИ** AYOLLAR HOJATXONASI
DISCOUNTS	**КАМАЙТИРИЛГАН НАРХЛАР** KAMAYTIRILGAN NARXLAR
SALE	**СОТИБ ТУГАТИШ** SOTIB TUGATISH
FREE	**БЕПУЛ** BEPUL
NEW!	**ЯНГИЛИК!** YANGILIK!
ATTENTION!	**ДИҚҚАТ!** DIQQAT!
NO VACANCIES	**ЖОЙ ЙЎҚ** JOY YO'Q
RESERVED	**БУЮРТМА ҚИЛИНГАН** BUYURTMA QILINGAN
ADMINISTRATION	**МАЪМУРИЯТ** MA'MURIYAT
STAFF ONLY	**ФАҚАТ ХОДИМЛАР УЧУН** FAQAT XODIMLAR UCHUN

BEWARE OF THE DOG!

ҚОПОНҒИЧ ИТ
QOPONG'ICH IT

NO SMOKING!

ЧЕКИЛМАСИН!
CHEKILMASIN!

DO NOT TOUCH!

ҚЎЛ БИЛАН ТЕГИЛМАСИН
QO'L BILAN TEGILMASIN

DANGEROUS

ХАТАРЛИ
XATARLI

DANGER

ХАТАР
XATAR

HIGH VOLTAGE

ЮҚОРИ КУЧЛАНИШ
YUQORI KUCHLANISH

NO SWIMMING!

ЧЎМИЛИШ ТАҚИҚЛАНГАН
CHO'MILISH TAQIQLANGAN

OUT OF ORDER

ИШЛАМАЙДИ
ISHLAMAYDI

FLAMMABLE

ЁНҒИНДАН ХАВФЛИ
YONG'INDAN XAVFLI

FORBIDDEN

ТАҚИҚЛАНГАН
TAQIQLANGAN

NO TRESPASSING!

ЎТИШ ТАҚИҚЛАНГАН
O'TISH TAQIQLANGAN

WET PAINT

БЎЯЛГАН
BO'YALGAN

CLOSED FOR RENOVATIONS

ТАЪМИРЛАШГА ЁПИЛГАН
TA'MIRLASHGA YOPILGAN

WORKS AHEAD

ТАЪМИРЛАШ ИШЛАРИ
TA'MIRLASH ISHLARI

DETOUR

АЙЛАНМА ЙЎЛ
AYLANMA YO'L

Transportation. General phrases

plane	**учоқ** uchoq
train	**поезд** poezd
bus	**автобус** avtobus
ferry	**паром** parom
taxi	**такси** taksi
car	**машина** mashina
schedule	**жадвал** jadval
Where can I see the schedule?	**Жадвални қаерда кўриш мумкин?** Jadvalni qaerda ko'rish mumkin?
workdays (weekdays)	**иш кунлари** ish kunlari
weekends	**дам олиш кунлари** dam olish kunlari
holidays	**байрам кунлари** bayram kunlari
DEPARTURE	**ЖЎНАШ** JO'NASH
ARRIVAL	**КЕЛИШ** KELISH
DELAYED	**УШЛАНИБ ҚОЛДИ** USHLANIB QOLDI
CANCELLED	**ҚОЛДИРИЛДИ** QOLDIRILDI
next (train, etc.)	**кейинги** keyingi
first	**биринчи** birinchi
last	**охирги** oxirgi
When is the next ...?	**Кейинги ... қачон бўлади?** Keyingi ... qachon bo'ladi?
When is the first ...?	**Биринчи ... қачон жўнайди?** Birinchi ... qachon jo'naydi?

When is the last …?

Охирги ... қачон жўнайди?
Oxirgi ... qachon jo'naydi?

transfer (change of trains, etc.)

бошқага ўтиш
boshqaga o'tish

to make a transfer

бошқага ўтиб олиш
boshqaga o'tib olish

Do I need to make a transfer?

Мен бошқага ўтиб олишим керакми?
Men boshqaga o'tib olishim kerakmi?

Buying tickets

Where can I buy tickets?	**Мен қаерда чипта сотиб олишим мумкин?** Men qaerda chipta sotib olishim mumkin?
ticket	**чипта** chipta
to buy a ticket	**чипта сотиб олиш** chipta sotib olish
ticket price	**чипта нархи** chipta narxi
Where to?	**Қаерга?** Qaerga?
To what station?	**Қайси бекатгача?** Qaysi bekatgacha?
I need ...	**Менга ... керак.** Menga ... kerak.
one ticket	**битта чипта** bitta chipta
two tickets	**иккита чипта** ikkita chipta
three tickets	**учта чипта** uchta chipta
one-way	**бир томонга** bir tomonga
round-trip	**бориб келишга** borib kelishga
first class	**биринчи класс** birinchi klass
second class	**иккинчи класс** ikkinchi klass
today	**бугун** bugun
tomorrow	**эртага** ertaga
the day after tomorrow	**эртадан кейин** ertadan keyin
in the morning	**эрталаб** ertalab
in the afternoon	**кундузи** kunduzi
in the evening	**кечқурун** kechqurun

aisle seat	**йўлак ёнидаги жой** yo'lak yonidagi joy
window seat	**дераза ёнидаги жой** deraza yonidagi joy
How much?	**Қанча?** Qancha?
Can I pay by credit card?	**Мен карточка билан тўлашим мумкинми?** Men kartochka bilan to'lashim mumkinmi?

Bus

bus	**автобус** avtobus
intercity bus	**шаҳарлараро автобус** shaharlararo avtobus
bus stop	**автобус бекати** avtobus bekati
Where's the nearest bus stop?	**Энг яқин автобус бекати қаерда?** Eng yaqin avtobus bekati qaerda?
number (bus ~, etc.)	**рақам** raqam
Which bus do I take to get to …?	**...гача қайси автобус боради?** ...gacha qaysi avtobus boradi?
Does this bus go to …?	**Бу автобус ...гача борадими?** Bu avtobus ...gacha boradimi?
How frequent are the buses?	**Автобуслар қанчалик тез юриб туради?** Avtobuslar qanchalik tez yurib turadi?
every 15 minutes	**ҳар ўн беш дақиқада** har o'n besh daqiqada
every half hour	**ҳар ярим соатда** har yarim soatda
every hour	**ҳар соатда** har soatda
several times a day	**кунига бир неча маротаба** kuniga bir necha marotaba
… times a day	**... маротаба кунига** ... marotaba kuniga
schedule	**жадвал** jadval
Where can I see the schedule?	**Жадвални қаерда кўриш мумкин?** Jadvalni qaerda ko'rish mumkin?
When is the next bus?	**Кейинги автобус қачон бўлади?** Keyingi avtobus qachon bo'ladi?
When is the first bus?	**Биринчи автобус қачон жўнайди?** Birinchi avtobus qachon jo'naydi?
When is the last bus?	**Охирги автобус қачон жўнайди?** Oxirgi avtobus qachon jo'naydi?
stop	**бекат** bekat

next stop	**кейинги бекат** keyingi bekat
last stop (terminus)	**охирги бекат** oxirgi bekat
Stop here, please.	**Шу ерда тўхтатинг, илтимос.** Shu erda to'xtating, iltimos.
Excuse me, this is my stop.	**Тўхтатворинг, бу менинг бекатим.** To'xtatvoring, bu mening bekatim.

Train

train	**поезд** poezd
suburban train	**шаҳар атрофига қатнайдиган поезд** shahar atrofiga qatnaydigan poezd
long-distance train	**ўзоққа қатнайдиган поезд** o'zoqqa qatnaydigan poezd
train station	**вокзал** vokzal
Excuse me, where is the exit to the platform?	**Кечирасиз, поездларга чиқиш қаерда?** Kechirasiz, poezdlarga chiqish qaerda?
Does this train go to …?	**Бу поезд …гача борадими?** Bu poezd …gacha boradimi?
next train	**кейинги поезд** keyingi poezd
When is the next train?	**Кейинги поезд қачон бўлади?** Keyingi poezd qachon bo'ladi?
Where can I see the schedule?	**Жадвални қаерда кўриш мумкин?** Jadvalni qaerda ko'rish mumkin?
From which platform?	**Қайси платформадан?** Qaysi platformadan?
When does the train arrive in …?	**Поезд …га қачон келади?** Poezd …ga qachon keladi?
Please help me.	**Ёрдам берворинг, илтимос.** Yordam bervoring, iltimos.
I'm looking for my seat.	**Мен ўз жойимни қидираяпман.** Men o'z joyimni qidirayapman.
We're looking for our seats.	**Биз жойларимизни қидираяпмиз.** Biz joylarimizni qidirayapmiz.
My seat is taken.	**Менинг жойим эгалланибди.** Mening joyim egallanibdi.
Our seats are taken.	**Жойларимиз эгалланибди.** Joylarimiz egallanibdi.
I'm sorry but this is my seat.	**Кечирасиз, аммо бу менинг жойим.** Kechirasiz, ammo bu mening joyim.
Is this seat taken?	**Бу жой бўшми?** Bu joy bo'shmi?
May I sit here?	**Мен бу ерса ўтира оламанми?** Men bu ersa o'tira olamanmi?

On the train. Dialogue (No ticket)

Ticket, please.

Чиптангизни кўрсатинг, илтимос.
Chiptangizni ko'rsating, iltimos.

I don't have a ticket.

Чиптам йўқ.
Chiptam yo'q.

I lost my ticket.

Мен чиптамни йўқотиб қўйдим.
Men chiptamni yo'qotib qo'ydim.

I forgot my ticket at home.

Мен чиптамни уйда қолдирибман.
Men chiptamni uyda qoldiribman.

You can buy a ticket from me.

Чиптани мендан сотиб олишингиз мумкин.
Chiptani mendan sotib olishingiz mumkin.

You will also have to pay a fine.

Сиз жарима тўлашингизга тўғри келади.
Siz jarima to'lashingizga to'g'ri keladi.

Okay.

Яхши.
Yaxshi.

Where are you going?

Қаерга кетаяпсиз?
Qaerga ketayapsiz?

I'm going to …

Мен ...гача кетаяпман.
Men ...gacha ketayapman.

How much? I don't understand.

Қанча? Тушунмаяпман.
Qancha? Tushunmayapman.

Write it down, please.

Ёзиб беринг, илтимос.
Yozib bering, iltimos.

Okay. Can I pay with a credit card?

Яхши. Мен карточка билан тўлашим мумкинми?
Yaxshi. Men kartochka bilan to'lashim mumkinmi?

Yes, you can.

Ҳа, мумкин.
Ha, mumkin.

Here's your receipt.

Бу сизнинг квитанциянгиз.
Bu sizning kvitantsiyangiz.

Sorry about the fine.

Жаримадан пушаймондаман.
Jarimadan pushaymondaman.

That's okay. It was my fault.

Ҳечқиси йўқ. Бу менинг айбим.
Hechqisi yo'q. Bu mening aybim.

Enjoy your trip.

Яхши етиб боринг.
Yaxshi etib boring.

Taxi

taxi	**такси** taksi
taxi driver	**таксичи** taksichi
to catch a taxi	**такси ушламоқ** taksi ushlamoq
taxi stand	**такси бекати** taksi bekati
Where can I get a taxi?	**Қаердан такси олишим мумкин?** Qaerdan taksi olishim mumkin?
to call a taxi	**такси чақирмоқ** taksi chaqirmoq
I need a taxi.	**Менга такси керак.** Menga taksi kerak.
Right now.	**Айнан ҳозир.** Aynan hozir.
What is your address (location)?	**Сизнинг манзилингиз?** Sizning manzilingiz?
My address is …	**Менинг манзилим …** Mening manzilim …
Your destination?	**Қаерга борасиз?** Qaerga borasiz?
Excuse me, …	**Кечирасиз, …** Kechirasiz, …
Are you available?	**Бўшмисиз?** Bo'shmisiz?
How much is it to get to …?	**…гача бориш қанча туради?** …gacha borish qancha turadi?
Do you know where it is?	**Қаерда эканини биласизми?** Qaerda ekanini bilasizmi?
Airport, please.	**Аэропортга, илтимос.** Aeroportga, iltimos.
Stop here, please.	**Шу ерда тўхтатинг, илтимос.** Shu erda to'xtating, iltimos.
It's not here.	**Бу ерда эмас.** Bu erda emas.
This is the wrong address.	**Бу нотўғри манзил.** Bu noto'g'ri manzil.

Turn left.	**Ҳозир чапга.**
	Hozir chapga.
Turn right.	**Ҳозир ўнгга.**
	Hozir o'ngga.

How much do I owe you?	**Сизга қанча беришим керак?**
	Sizga qancha berishim kerak?
I'd like a receipt, please.	**Менга чекни беринг, илтимос.**
	Menga chekni bering, iltimos.
Keep the change.	**Қайтими кераги йўқ.**
	Qaytimi keragi yo'q.

Would you please wait for me?	**Мени кутиб туринг, илтимос.**
	Meni kutib turing, iltimos.
five minutes	**беш дақиқа**
	besh daqiqa
ten minutes	**ўн дақиқа**
	o'n daqiqa
fifteen minutes	**ўн беш дақиқа**
	o'n besh daqiqa
twenty minutes	**йигирма дақиқа**
	yigirma daqiqa
half an hour	**ярим соат**
	yarim soat

Hotel

Hello.	**Ассалому алайкум.** Assalomu alaykum.
My name is …	**Менинг исмим …** Mening ismim …
I have a reservation.	**Мен хона банд қилган эдим.** Men xona band qilgan edim.
I need …	**Менга … керак.** Menga … kerak.
a single room	**бир ўринли хона** bir o'rinli xona
a double room	**икки ўринли хона** ikki o'rinli xona
How much is that?	**Қанча туради?** Qancha turadi?
That's a bit expensive.	**Бу бироз қиммат.** Bu biroz qimmat.
Do you have anything else?	**Сизда яна бирор нарса борми?** Sizda yana biror narsa bormi?
I'll take it.	**Мен уни оламан.** Men uni olaman.
I'll pay in cash.	**Мен нақд тўлайман.** Men naqd to'layman.
I've got a problem.	**Менда бир муаммо бор.** Menda bir muammo bor.
My … is broken.	**Менинг … бузилган.** Mening … buzilgan.
My … is out of order.	**Менда … ишламаяпти** Menda … ishlamayapti
TV	**телевизор** televizor
air conditioner	**кондиционер** konditsioner
tap	**кран** kran
shower	**душ** dush
sink	**чаноқ** chanoq
safe	**сейф** seyf

door lock	**қулф** qulf
electrical outlet	**розетка** rozetka
hairdryer	**фен** fen
I don't have …	**Менда ... йўқ.** Menda ... yo'q.
water	**сув** suv
light	**нур** nur
electricity	**электр ёруғи** elektr yorug'i
Can you give me …?	**Менга ... бера оласизми?** Menga ... bera olasizmi?
a towel	**сочиқ** sochiq
a blanket	**адёл** adyol
slippers	**шиппак** shippak
a robe	**халат** xalat
shampoo	**шампун** shampun
soap	**совун** sovun
I'd like to change rooms.	**Мен хонани алмаштирмоқчи эдим.** Men xonani almashtirmoqchi edim.
I can't find my key.	**Мен калитимни топа олмаяпман.** Men kalitimni topa olmayapman.
Could you open my room, please?	**Менга хонани очиб беринг, илтимос.** Menga xonani ochib bering, iltimos.
Who's there?	**Ким у?** Kim u?
Come in!	**Киринг!** Kiring!
Just a minute!	**Бир дақиқа!** Bir daqiqa!
Not right now, please.	**Узр, ҳозир эмас.** Uzr, hozir emas.
Come to my room, please.	**Хонамга киринг, илтимос.** Xonamga kiring, iltimos.
I'd like to order food service.	**Мен хонамга егулик буюрмоқчи эдим.** Men xonamga egulik buyurmoqchi edim.

My room number is …	**Хонамнинг рақами …** Xonamning raqami …
I'm leaving …	**Мен … кетаяпман.** Men … ketayapman.
We're leaving …	**Биз … кетаяпмиз.** Biz … ketayapmiz.
right now	**ҳозир** hozir
this afternoon	**бугун тушликдан кейин** bugun tushlikdan keyin
tonight	**бугун кечқурун** bugun kechqurun
tomorrow	**эртага** ertaga
tomorrow morning	**эртага эрталаб** ertaga ertalab
tomorrow evening	**эртага кечқурун** ertaga kechqurun
the day after tomorrow	**эртадан кейин** ertadan keyin

I'd like to pay.	**Мен сиз билан ҳисоб-китоб қилмоқчиман.** Men siz bilan hisob-kitob qilmoqchiman.
Everything was wonderful.	**Ҳаммаси аъло даражада эди.** Hammasi a'lo darajada edi.
Where can I get a taxi?	**Қаердан такси олишим мумкин?** Qaerdan taksi olishim mumkin?
Would you call a taxi for me, please?	**Менга такси чақиртиринг, илтимос.** Menga taksi chaqirtiring, iltimos.

Restaurant

Can I look at the menu, please?	**Таомномангизни кўришим мумкинми?** Taomnomangizni ko'rishim mumkinmi?
Table for one.	**Бир кишилик жой.** Bir kishilik joy.
There are two (three, four) of us.	**Икки (уч, тўрт) кишимиз.** Ikki (uch, to'rt) kishimiz.
Smoking	**Чекувчилар учун** Chekuvchilar uchun
No smoking	**Чекмайдиганлар учун** Chekmaydiganlar uchun
Excuse me! (addressing a waiter)	**Маъзур тутасиз!** Ma'zur tutasiz!
menu	**таомнома** taomnoma
wine list	**винолар картаси** vinolar kartasi
The menu, please.	**Таомнома беринг, илтимос.** Taomnoma bering, iltimos.
Are you ready to order?	**Буюртма беришга тайёрмисиз?** Buyurtma berishga tayyormisiz?
What will you have?	**Нима буюрасиз?** Nima buyurasiz?
I'll have …	**Мен … хоҳлайман.** Men … xohlayman.
I'm a vegetarian.	**Мен вегетариан.** Men vegetarian.
meat	**гўшт** go'sht
fish	**балиқ** baliq
vegetables	**сабзавот** sabzavot
Do you have vegetarian dishes?	**Вегетариан таомларингиз борми?** Vegetarian taomlaringiz bormi?
I don't eat pork.	**Мен чўчқа гўштини емайман.** Men cho'chqa go'shtini emayman.
He /she/ doesn't eat meat.	**У гўшт емайди.** U go'sht emaydi.
I am allergic to …	**Менда …га аллергия бор.** Menda …ga allergiya bor.

Would you please bring me ...	**Менга ... келтиринг, илтимос.** Menga ... keltiring, iltimos.
salt | pepper | sugar	**туз | қалампир | шакар** tuz | qalampir | shakar
coffee | tea | dessert	**кофе | чой| ширинлик** kofe | choy | shirinlik
water | sparkling | plain	**сув | газли | газсиз** suv | gazli | gazsiz
a spoon | fork | knife	**қошиқ | санчқи | пичоқ** qoshiq | sanchqi | pichoq
a plate | napkin	**ликопча | салфетка** likopcha | salfetka

Enjoy your meal!	**Ёқимли иштаҳа!** Yoqimli ishtaha!
One more, please.	**Яна олиб келинг, илтимос.** Yana olib keling, iltimos.
It was very delicious.	**Жуда мазали экан.** Juda mazali ekan.

check | change | tip	**ҳисоб | қайтим | чойчақа** hisob | qaytim | choychaqa
Check, please. (Could I have the check, please?)	**Ҳисобни келтиринг, илтимос.** Hisobni keltiring, iltimos.
Can I pay by credit card?	**Мен карточка билан тўлашим мумкинми?** Men kartochka bilan to'lashim mumkinmi?
I'm sorry, there's a mistake here.	**Кечирасиз, бу ерда хато бор.** Kechirasiz, bu erda xato bor.

Shopping

Can I help you?	**Сизга ёрдам бера оламанми?** Sizga yordam bera olamanmi?
Do you have …?	**Сизда … борми?** Sizda … bormi?
I'm looking for …	**Мен … қидираяпман.** Men … qidirayapman.
I need …	**Менга … керак.** Menga … kerak.
I'm just looking.	**Мен шунчаки томоша қилаяпман.** Men shunchaki tomosha qilayapman.
We're just looking.	**Биз шунчаки томоша қилаяпмиз.** Biz shunchaki tomosha qilayapmiz.
I'll come back later.	**Кейинроқ кираман.** Keyinroq kiraman.
We'll come back later.	**Биз кейинроқ кирамиз.** Biz keyinroq kiramiz.
discounts | sale	**камайтирилган нархлар | сотиб тугатиш** kamaytirilgan narxlar | sotib tugatish
Would you please show me …	**Илтимос, менга … кўрсатинг.** Iltimos, menga … ko'rsating.
Would you please give me …	**Илтимос, менга … беринг.** Iltimos, menga … bering.
Can I try it on?	**Мен буни кийиб кўрсам бўладими?** Men buni kiyib ko'rsam bo'ladimi?
Excuse me, where's the fitting room?	**Кечирасиз, кийиб кўриш хонаси қаерда?** Kechirasiz, kiyib ko'rish xonasi qaerda?
Which color would you like?	**Қайси рангни истайсиз?** Qaysi rangni istaysiz?
size | length	**размер | бўй** razmer | bo'y
How does it fit?	**Тўғри келдими?** To'g'ri keldimi?
How much is it?	**Бу қанча туради?** Bu qancha turadi?
That's too expensive.	**Бу жуда қиммат.** Bu juda qimmat.
I'll take it.	**Мен буни оламан.** Men buni olaman.

Excuse me, where do I pay?

Кечирасиз, касса қаерда?
Kechirasiz, kassa qaerda?

Will you pay in cash or credit card?

Сиз қандай тўлайсиз? Нақдми карточка биланми?
Siz qanday to'laysiz? Naqdmi kartochka bilanmi?

In cash | with credit card

нақд | карточка
naqd | kartochka

Do you want the receipt?

Сизга чек керакми?
Sizga chek kerakmi?

Yes, please.

Ҳа, илтимос.
Ha, iltimos.

No, it's OK.

Йўқ, кераги йўқ. Раҳмат.
Yo'q, keragi yo'q. Rahmat.

Thank you. Have a nice day!

Раҳмат. Ишларингизга омад!
Rahmat. Ishlaringizga omad!

In town

Excuse me, …	**Кечирасиз, илтимос …** Kechirasiz, iltimos …
I'm looking for …	**Мен … қидираяпман.** Men … qidirayapman.
the subway	**метро** metro
my hotel	**ўз меҳмонхонамни** o'z mehmonxonamni
the movie theater	**кинотеатр** kinoteatr
a taxi stand	**такси бекатини** taksi bekatini
an ATM	**банкомат** bankomat
a foreign exchange office	**валюта алмаштириш жойини** valyuta almashtirish joyini
an internet café	**интернет-кафе** internet-kafe
… street	**… кўчасини** … ko'chasini
this place	**мана бу жойни** mana bu joyni
Do you know where … is?	**Сиз … қаерда жойлашганини билмайсизми?** Siz … qaerda joylashganini bilmaysizmi?
Which street is this?	**Бу кўча нима деб номланади?** Bu ko'cha nima deb nomlanadi?
Show me where we are right now.	**Ҳозир қаерда эканимизни кўрсатиб юборинг.** Hozir qaerda ekanimizni ko'rsatib yuboring.
Can I get there on foot?	**У ерга пиёда бора оламанми?** U erga piyoda bora olamanmi?
Do you have a map of the city?	**Сизда шаҳар харитаси борми?** Sizda shahar xaritasi bormi?
How much is a ticket to get in?	**Кириш чиптаси неча пул туради?** Kirish chiptasi necha pul turadi?
Can I take pictures here?	**Бу ерда суратга тушиш мумкинми?** Bu erda suratga tushish mumkinmi?

Are you open?	**Очиқмисиз?**
	Ochiqmisiz?
When do you open?	**Соат нечада очасиз?**
	Soat nechada ochasiz?
When do you close?	**Соат нечагача ишлайсиз?**
	Soat nechagacha ishlaysiz?

Money

money	**пул** pul
cash	**нақд пул** naqd pul
paper money	**қоғоз пул** qog'oz pul
loose change	**чақа** chaqa
check | change | tip	**ҳисоб | қайтим | чойчақа** hisob | qaytim | choychaqa
credit card	**кредит карточкаси** kredit kartochkasi
wallet	**ҳамён** hamyon
to buy	**сотиб олмоқ** sotib olmoq
to pay	**тўламоқ** to'lamoq
fine	**жарима** jarima
free	**бепул** bepul
Where can I buy ...?	**Мен қаерда ... сотиб олишим мумкин?** Men qaerda ... sotib olishim mumkin?
Is the bank open now?	**Банк ҳозир очиқми?** Bank hozir ochiqmi?
When does it open?	**Соат нечада у очилади?** Soat nechada u ochiladi?
When does it close?	**Соат нечагача у ишлайди?** Soat nechagacha u ishlaydi?
How much?	**Қанча?** Qancha?
How much is this?	**Бу қанча туради?** Bu qancha turadi?
That's too expensive.	**Бу жуда қиммат.** Bu juda qimmat.
Excuse me, where do I pay?	**Кечирасиз, касса қаерда?** Kechirasiz, kassa qaerda?

Check, please.

Ҳисобни келтиринг, илтимос.
Hisobni keltiring, iltimos.

Can I pay by credit card?

Мен карточка билан тўлашим мумкинми?
Men kartochka bilan to'lashim mumkinmi?

Is there an ATM here?

Бу ерда банкомат борми?
Bu erda bankomat bormi?

I'm looking for an ATM.

Менга банкомат керак.
Menga bankomat kerak.

I'm looking for a foreign exchange office.

Мен пул алмаштирадиган жой қидираяпман.
Men pul almashtiradigan joy qidirayapman.

I'd like to change ...

Мен ... алмаштириб олмоқчиман.
Men ... almashtirib olmoqchiman.

What is the exchange rate?

Алмаштириш курси қанақа?
Almashtirish kursi qanaqa?

Do you need my passport?

Сизга паспортим керакми?
Sizga pasportim kerakmi?

Time

What time is it?	**Соат неча бўлди?** Soat necha bo'ldi?
When?	**Қачон?** Qachon?
At what time?	**Соат нечада?** Soat nechada?
now | later | after …	**ҳозир | кейинроқ | кейин …** hozir | keyinroq | keyin …
one o'clock	**кундузги бир** kunduzgi bir
one fifteen	**биру ўн беш** biru o'n besh
one thirty	**биру ўттиз** biru o'ttiz
one forty-five	**ўн бешта кам икки** o'n beshta kam ikki
one | two | three	**бир | икки | уч** bir | ikki | uch
four | five | six	**тўрт | беш | олти** to'rt | besh | olti
seven | eight | nine	**етти | саккиз | тўққиз** etti | sakkiz | to'qqiz
ten | eleven | twelve	**ўн | ўн бир | ўн икки** o'n | o'n bir | o'n ikki
in …	**… дан кейин** … dan keyin
five minutes	**беш дақиқа** besh daqiqa
ten minutes	**ўн дақиқа** o'n daqiqa
fifteen minutes	**ўн беш дақиқа** o'n besh daqiqa
twenty minutes	**йигирма дақиқа** yigirma daqiqa
half an hour	**ярим соат** yarim soat
an hour	**бир соат** bir soat

in the morning	**эрталаб** ertalab
early in the morning	**тонг саҳарда** tong saharda
this morning	**бугун эрталаб** bugun ertalab
tomorrow morning	**эртага эрталаб** ertaga ertalab
in the middle of the day	**тушлик пайтида** tushlik paytida
in the afternoon	**тушликдан кейин** tushlikdan keyin
in the evening	**кечқурун** kechqurun
tonight	**бугун кечқурун** bugun kechqurun
at night	**кечаси** kechasi
yesterday	**кеча** kecha
today	**бугун** bugun
tomorrow	**эртага** ertaga
the day after tomorrow	**эртадан кейин** ertadan keyin
What day is it today?	**Бугун қайси кун?** Bugun qaysi kun?
It's ...	**Бугун ...** Bugun ...
Monday	**душанба** dushanba
Tuesday	**сешанба** seshanba
Wednesday	**чоршанба** chorshanba
Thursday	**пайшанба** payshanba
Friday	**жума** juma
Saturday	**шанба** shanba
Sunday	**якшанба** yakshanba

Greetings. Introductions

Hello.	**Ассалому алайкум.** Assalomu alaykum.
Pleased to meet you.	**Танишганимдан хурсандман.** Tanishganimdan xursandman.
Me too.	**Мен ҳам.** Men ham.
I'd like you to meet …	**Танишинг. Бу …** Tanishing. Bu …
Nice to meet you.	**Жуда хурсандман.** Juda xursandman.
How are you?	**Қалайсиз? Ишларингиз қалай?** Qalaysiz? Ishlaringiz qalay?
My name is …	**Менинг исмим …** Mening ismim …
His name is …	**Унинг исми …** Uning ismi …
Her name is …	**Унинг исми …** Uning ismi …
What's your name?	**Исмингиз нима?** Ismingiz nima?
What's his name?	**Унинг исми нима?** Uning ismi nima?
What's her name?	**Унинг исми нима?** Uning ismi nima?
What's your last name?	**Фамилиянгиз нима?** Familiyangiz nima?
You can call me …	**Мени … деб чақиришингиз мумкин.** Meni … deb chaqirishingiz mumkin.
Where are you from?	**Қаердансиз?** Qaerdansiz?
I'm from …	**Мен …дан.** Men …dan.
What do you do for a living?	**Ким бўлиб ишлайсиз?** Kim bo'lib ishlaysiz?
Who is this?	**Ким бу?** Kim bu?
Who is he?	**Ким у?** Kim u?
Who is she?	**Ким у?** Kim u?
Who are they?	**Ким улар?** Kim ular?

This is …

Бу …
Bu …

my friend (masc.)

менинг дўстим
mening do'stim

my friend (fem.)

менинг дугонам
mening dugonam

my husband

менинг эрим
mening erim

my wife

менинг рафиқам
mening rafiqam

my father

менинг отам
mening otam

my mother

менинг онам
mening onam

my brother

менинг акам
mening akam

my sister

менинг синглим
mening singlim

my son

менинг ўғлим
mening o'g'lim

my daughter

менинг қизим
mening qizim

This is our son.

Бу бизнинг ўғлимиз.
Bu bizning o'g'limiz.

This is our daughter.

Бу бизнинг қизимиз.
Bu bizning qizimiz.

These are my children.

Бу менинг болаларим.
Bu mening bolalarim.

These are our children.

Бу бизнинг болаларимиз.
Bu bizning bolalarimiz.

Farewells

Good bye!	**Кўришгунча!** Ko'rishguncha!
Bye! (inform.)	**Хайр!** Xayr!
See you tomorrow.	**Эртагача.** Ertagacha.
See you soon.	**Учрашгунча.** Uchrashguncha.
See you at seven.	**Соат еттида учрашамиз.** Soat ettida uchrashamiz.
Have fun!	**Дам олинг!** Dam oling!
Talk to you later.	**Кейинроқ гаплашамиз.** Keyinroq gaplashamiz.
Have a nice weekend.	**Дам олиш кунларини яхши ўтказинг.** Dam olish kunlarini yaxshi o'tkazing.
Good night.	**Хайрли кеч.** Xayrli kech.
It's time for me to go.	**Вақт бўлди.** Vaqt bo'ldi.
I have to go.	**Боришим керак.** Borishim kerak.
I will be right back.	**Ҳозир қайтиб келаман.** Hozir qaytib kelaman.
It's late.	**Кеч бўлди.** Kech bo'ldi.
I have to get up early.	**Барвақт туришим керак.** Barvaqt turishim kerak.
I'm leaving tomorrow.	**Мен эртага кетаман.** Men ertaga ketaman.
We're leaving tomorrow.	**Биз эртага кетамиз.** Biz ertaga ketamiz.
Have a nice trip!	**Оқ йўл!** Oq yo'l!
It was nice meeting you.	**Танишганимдан хурсандман.** Tanishganimdan xursandman.
It was nice talking to you.	**Сиз билан гаплашгандан хурсандман.** Siz bilan gaplashgandan xursandman.

Thanks for everything.	**Ҳаммаси учун раҳмат.**
	Hammasi uchun rahmat.
I had a very good time.	**Мен ажойиб вақт ўтказдим.**
	Men ajoyib vaqt o'tkazdim.
We had a very good time.	**Биз ажойиб вақт ўтказдик.**
	Biz ajoyib vaqt o'tkazdik.
It was really great.	**Ҳаммаси ажойиб.**
	Hammasi ajoyib.
I'm going to miss you.	**Соғиниб қоламан.**
	Sog'inib qolaman.
We're going to miss you.	**Соғиниб қоламиз.**
	Sog'inib qolamiz.

Good luck!	**Омад! Яхши қолинг!**
	Omad! Yaxshi qoling!
Say hi to …	**...га салом айтинг!**
	...ga salom ayting!

Foreign language

I don't understand.	**Мен тушунмаяпман.** Men tushunmayapman.
Write it down, please.	**Буни ёзиб беринг.** Buni yozib bering.
Do you speak …?	**Сиз …чани биласизми?** Siz …chani bilasizmi?
I speak a little bit of …	**Мен бироз …ча биламан.** Men biroz …cha bilaman.
English	**инглиз** ingliz
Turkish	**турк** turk
Arabic	**араб** arab
French	**француз** frantsuz
German	**немис** nemis
Italian	**италян** italyan
Spanish	**испан** ispan
Portuguese	**португал** portugal
Chinese	**хитой** xitoy
Japanese	**япон** yapon
Can you repeat that, please.	**Такрорлаб юборинг, илтимос.** Takrorlab yuboring, iltimos.
I understand.	**Тушундим.** Tushundim.
I don't understand.	**Мен тушунмаяпман.** Men tushunmayapman.
Please speak more slowly.	**Секинроқ гапиринг, илтимос.** Sekinroq gapiring, iltimos.
Is that correct? (Am I saying it right?)	**Бу тўғрими?** Bu to'g'rimi?
What is this? (What does this mean?)	**Бу нима?** Bu nima?

Apologies

Excuse me, please.	**Кечиринг, илтимос.** Kechiring, iltimos.
I'm sorry.	**Мен пушаймон еяпман.** Men pushaymon eyapman.
I'm really sorry.	**Ачинарли ҳол.** Achinarli hol.
Sorry, it's my fault.	**Айбдорман, бу менинг айбим.** Aybdorman, bu mening aybim.
My mistake.	**Менинг айбим.** Mening aybim.
May I ...?	**... қила оламанми?** ... qila olamanmi?
Do you mind if I ...?	**Агарда мен ... қарши эмасмисиз?** Agarda men ... qarshi emasmisiz?
It's OK.	**Ҳечқиси йўқ.** Hechqisi yo'q.
It's all right.	**Ҳаммаси жойида.** Hammasi joyida.
Don't worry about it.	**Ташвишланманг.** Tashvishlanmang.

Agreement

Yes.

Ҳа.
Ha.

Yes, sure.

Ҳа, албатта.
Ha, albatta.

OK (Good!)

Яхши!
Yaxshi!

Very well.

Жуда яхши.
Juda yaxshi.

Certainly!

Албатта!
Albatta!

I agree.

Мен розиман.
Men roziman.

That's correct.

Тўғри.
To'g'ri.

That's right.

Худди шундай.
Xuddi shunday.

You're right.

Ҳақсиз.
Haqsiz.

I don't mind.

Қарши эмасман.
Qarshi emasman.

Absolutely right.

Мутлақо тўғри.
Mutlaqo to'g'ri.

It's possible.

Бу мумкин.
Bu mumkin.

That's a good idea.

Бу яхши фикр.
Bu yaxshi fikr.

I can't say no.

Рад жавобини бера олмайман.
Rad javobini bera olmayman.

I'd be happy to.

Хурсанд бўлар эдим.
Xursand bo'lar edim.

With pleasure.

Жоним билан.
Jonim bilan.

Refusal. Expressing doubt

No.

Йўқ.
Yo'q.

Certainly not.

Албатта йўқ.
Albatta yo'q.

I don't agree.

Мен рози эмасман.
Men rozi emasman.

I don't think so.

Мен бундай деб ўйламайман.
Men bunday deb o'ylamayman.

It's not true.

Бу нотўғри.
Bu noto'g'ri.

You are wrong.

Сиз ноҳақ.
Siz nohaq.

I think you are wrong.

Сиз ноҳақсиз, деб ўйлайман.
Siz nohaqsiz, deb o'ylayman.

I'm not sure.

Иккиланаяпман.
Ikkilanayapman.

It's impossible.

Бунинг бўлиши мумкин эмас.
Buning bo'lishi mumkin emas.

Nothing of the kind (sort)!

Асло ундай эмас!
Aslo unday emas!

The exact opposite.

Аксинча!
Aksincha!

I'm against it.

Мен қаршиман.
Men qarshiman.

I don't care.

Менга барибир.
Menga baribir.

I have no idea.

Билмайман.
Bilmayman.

I doubt it.

Бундай бўлишига шубҳам бор.
Bunday bo'lishiga shubham bor.

Sorry, I can't.

Кечирасиз, имконим йўқ.
Kechirasiz, imkonim yo'q.

Sorry, I don't want to.

Кечирасиз, мен истамайман.
Kechirasiz, men istamayman.

Thank you, but I don't need this.

Раҳмат, бунинг менга кераги йўқ.
Rahmat, buning menga keragi yo'q.

It's getting late.

Кеч бўлди.
Kech bo'ldi.

I have to get up early.	**Барвақт туришим керак.** Barvaqt turishim kerak.
I don't feel well.	**Ўзимни ёмон ҳис этаяпман.** O'zimni yomon his etayapman.

Expressing gratitude

Thank you. | **Раҳмат.**
Rahmat.

Thank you very much. | **Катта раҳмат.**
Katta rahmat.

I really appreciate it. | **Ташаккур.**
Tashakkur.

I'm really grateful to you. | **Сиздан миннатдорман.**
Sizdan minnatdorman.

We are really grateful to you. | **Сиздан миннатдормиз.**
Sizdan minnatdormiz.

Thank you for your time. | **Вақтингизни сарфлаганингиз учун ташаккур.**
Vaqtingizni sarflaganingiz uchun tashakkur.

Thanks for everything. | **Ҳаммаси учун раҳмат.**
Hammasi uchun rahmat.

Thank you for ... | **... учун раҳмат.**
... uchun rahmat.

your help | **Ёрдамингиз**
Yordamingiz

a nice time | **яхши вақт ўтказганимиз**
yaxshi vaqt o'tkazganimiz

a wonderful meal | **ажойиб овқат**
ajoyib ovqat

a pleasant evening | **мароқли оқшом**
maroqli oqshom

a wonderful day | **ғаройиб кун**
g'aroyib kun

an amazing journey | **қизиқарли экскурсия**
qiziqarli ekskursiya

Don't mention it. | **Арзимайди.**
Arzimaydi.

You are welcome. | **Миннатдорчиликка арзимайди.**
Minnatdorchilikka arzimaydi.

Any time. | **Марҳамат қилинг.**
Marhamat qiling.

My pleasure. | **Ёрдамим текканидан хурсандман.**
Yordamim tekkanidan xursandman.

Forget it.

Эсдан чиқаринг. Ҳаммаси жойида.
Esdan chiqaring. Hammasi joyida.

Don't worry about it.

Ташвишланманг.
Tashvishlanmang.

Congratulations. Best wishes

Congratulations!	**Табриклайман!** Tabriklayman!
Happy birthday!	**Туғилган кунингиз билан!** Tug'ilgan kuningiz bilan!
Merry Christmas!	**Рождество муборак!** Rojdestvo muborak!
Happy New Year!	**Янги йилингиз билан!** Yangi yilingiz bilan!
Happy Easter!	**Ёрқин Пасха муборак!** Yorqin Pasxa muborak!
Happy Hanukkah!	**Хайрли Хануки!** Xayrli Xanuki!
I'd like to propose a toast.	**Менда тост бор.** Menda tost bor.
Cheers!	**Соғлигингиз учун!** Sog'ligingiz uchun!
Let's drink to …!	**… учун ичайлик!** … uchun ichaylik!
To our success!	**Омадимиз учун!** Omadimiz uchun!
To your success!	**Омадингиз учун!** Omadingiz uchun!
Good luck!	**Омад!** Omad!
Have a nice day!	**Хайрли кун!** Xayrli kun!
Have a good holiday!	**Яхши дам олинг!** Yaxshi dam oling!
Have a safe journey!	**Оқ йўл!** Oq yo'l!
I hope you get better soon!	**Тезроқ соғайиб кетинг!** Tezroq sog'ayib keting!

Socializing

Why are you sad?	**Нимадан хафасиз?** Nimadan xafasiz?
Smile! Cheer up!	**Жилмайинг!** Jilmaying!
Are you free tonight?	**Бугун кечга бўшмисиз?** Bugun kechga bo'shmisiz?
May I offer you a drink?	**Сизга ичиш таклиф эта оламанми?** Sizga ichish taklif eta olamanmi?
Would you like to dance?	**Рақсга тушмайсизми?** Raqsga tushmaysizmi?
Let's go to the movies.	**Балким кинога борармиз?** Balkim kinoga borarmiz?
May I invite you to …?	**Сизни …га таклиф этишим мумкинми?** Sizni …ga taklif etishim mumkinmi?
a restaurant	**ресторан** restoran
the movies	**кино** kino
the theater	**театр** teatr
go for a walk	**сайр** sayr
At what time?	**Соат нечада?** Soat nechada?
tonight	**бугун кечга** bugun kechga
at six	**соат олтига** soat oltiga
at seven	**соат еттига** soat ettiga
at eight	**соат саккизга** soat sakkizga
at nine	**соат тўққизга** soat to'qqizga
Do you like it here?	**Сизга бу ер ёқадими?** Sizga bu er yoqadimi?
Are you here with someone?	**Сиз бу ерда ким биландирмисиз?** Siz bu erda kim bilandirmisiz?

I'm with my friend.	**Мен дўстим /дугонам/ билан.**
	Men do'stim /dugonam/ bilan.
I'm with my friends.	**Мен дўстларим билан.**
	Men do'stlarim bilan.
No, I'm alone.	**Мен бир ўзим.**
	Men bir o'zim.

Do you have a boyfriend?	**Сенда дўстинг борми?**
	Senda do'sting bormi?
I have a boyfriend.	**Менда дўстим бор.**
	Menda do'stim bor.
Do you have a girlfriend?	**Сенда яхши кўрган қизинг борми?**
	Senda yaxshi ko'rgan qizing bormi?
I have a girlfriend.	**Менда яхши кўрган қизим бор.**
	Menda yaxshi ko'rgan qizim bor.

Can I see you again?	**Биз яна учрашамизми?**
	Biz yana uchrashamizmi?
Can I call you?	**Сенга қўнғироқ қилсам бўладими?**
	Senga qo'ng'iroq qilsam bo'ladimi?
Call me. (Give me a call.)	**Менга қўнғироқ қил.**
	Menga qo'ng'iroq qil.
What's your number?	**Рақамларинг қанақа?**
	Raqamlaring qanaqa?
I miss you.	**Мен сени соғимдим.**
	Men seni sog'imdim.

You have a beautiful name.	**Исмингиз жуда чиройли экан.**
	Ismingiz juda chiroyli ekan.
I love you.	**Мен сени севаман.**
	Men seni sevaman.
Will you marry me?	**Менга турмушга чиқ.**
	Menga turmushga chiq.
You're kidding!	**Ҳазиллашаяпсиз!**
	Hazillashayapsiz!
I'm just kidding.	**Мен шунчаки ҳазиллашаяпман.**
	Men shunchaki hazillashayapman.

Are you serious?	**Жиддий гапираяпсизми?**
	Jiddiy gapirayapsizmi?
I'm serious.	**Жиддий гапираяпман.**
	Jiddiy gapirayapman.
Really?!	**Ростми?!**
	Rostmi?!
It's unbelievable!	**Бунинг бўлиши мумкин эмас!**
	Buning bo'lishi mumkin emas!
I don't believe you.	**Сизга ишонмайман.**
	Sizga ishonmayman.
I can't.	**Мен қила олмайман.**
	Men qila olmayman.
I don't know.	**Билмайман.**
	Bilmayman.

I don't understand you.

Мен сизни тушунмаяпман.
Men sizni tushunmayapman.

Please go away.

Кетинг, илтимос.
Keting, iltimos.

Leave me alone!

Мени тинч қўйинг!
Meni tinch qo'ying!

I can't stand him.

Мен уни кўра олмайман.
Men uni ko'ra olmayman.

You are disgusting!

Сиз жирканчсиз!
Siz jirkanchsiz!

I'll call the police!

Мен полиция чақиртираман!
Men politsiya chaqirtiraman!

Sharing impressions. Emotions

I like it.	**Менга бу ёқаяпти.**
	Menga bu yoqayapti.
Very nice.	**Жуда ёқимли.**
	Juda yoqimli.
That's great!	**Бу зўр!**
	Bu zo'r!
It's not bad.	**Ёмон эмас.**
	Yomon emas.

I don't like it.	**Менга бу ёқмаяпти.**
	Menga bu yoqmayapti.
It's not good.	**Бу яхши эмас.**
	Bu yaxshi emas.
It's bad.	**Бу ёмон.**
	Bu yomon.
It's very bad.	**Бу жуда ёмон.**
	Bu juda yomon.
It's disgusting.	**Бу жирканч.**
	Bu jirkanch.

I'm happy.	**Мен бахтлиман.**
	Men baxtliman.
I'm content.	**Мен мамнунман.**
	Men mamnunman.
I'm in love.	**Мен севиб қолдим.**
	Men sevib qoldim.
I'm calm.	**Мен тинчман.**
	Men tinchman.
I'm bored.	**Менга зерикарли.**
	Menga zerikarli.

I'm tired.	**Мен чарчадим.**
	Men charchadim.
I'm sad.	**Мен хафаман.**
	Men xafaman.
I'm frightened.	**Мен қўрқиб кетдим.**
	Men qo'rqib ketdim.

I'm angry.	**Жаҳлим чиқаяпти.**
	Jahlim chiqayapti.
I'm worried.	**Мен ҳаяжондаман.**
	Men hayajondaman.
I'm nervous.	**Мен асабийлашаяпман.**
	Men asabiylashayapman.

I'm jealous. (envious)	**Мен ҳасад қилаяпман.** Men hasad qilayapman.
I'm surprised.	**Мен ҳайронман.** Men hayronman.
I'm perplexed.	**Бошим қотиб қолди.** Boshim qotib qoldi.

Problems. Accidents

I've got a problem.	**Менда бир муаммо бор.** Menda bir muammo bor.
We've got a problem.	**Бизда муаммо бор.** Bizda muammo bor.
I'm lost.	**Мен адашиб қолдим.** Men adashib qoldim.
I missed the last bus (train).	**Мен охирги автобусга (поездга) кеч қолдим.** Men oxirgi avtobusga (poezdga) kech qoldim.
I don't have any money left.	**Менда умуман пулим қолмади.** Menda umuman pulim qolmadi.
I've lost my ...	**Мен ... йўқотиб қўйдим.** Men ... yo'qotib qo'ydim.
Someone stole my ...	**Менда ...ни ўғирлашди.** Menda ...ni o'g'irlashdi.
passport	**паспорт** pasport
wallet	**ҳамён** hamyon
papers	**ҳужжат** hujjat
ticket	**чипта** chipta
money	**пул** pul
handbag	**сумка** sumka
camera	**фотоаппарат** fotoapparat
laptop	**ноутбук** noutbuk
tablet computer	**планшет** planshet
mobile phone	**телефон** telefon
Help me!	**Ёрдам беринг!** Yordam bering!
What's happened?	**Нима бўлди?** Nima bo'ldi?

fire	**ёнғин** yong'in
shooting	**отишма** otishma
murder	**қотиллик** qotillik
explosion	**портлаш** portlash
fight	**муштлашув** mushtlashuv

Call the police!	**Полиция чақиртиринг!** Politsiya chaqirtiring!
Please hurry up!	**Илтимос, тезроқ!** Iltimos, tezroq!
I'm looking for the police station.	**Мен полиция участкасини қидираяпман.** Men politsiya uchastkasini qidirayapman.
I need to make a call.	**Қўнғироқ қилишим керак.** Qo'ng'iroq qilishim kerak.
May I use your phone?	**Қўнғироқ қилсам бўладими?** Qo'ng'iroq qilsam bo'ladimi?

I've been …	**Мени …** Meni …
mugged	**тунашди** tunashdi
robbed	**ўғирлашди** o'g'irlashdi
raped	**зўрлашди** zo'rlashdi
attacked (beaten up)	**калтаклашди** kaltaklashdi

Are you all right?	**Аҳволингиз яхшими?** Ahvolingiz yaxshimi?
Did you see who it was?	**Сиз улар кимлигини кўрдингизми?** Siz ular kimligini ko'rdingizmi?
Would you be able to recognize the person?	**Сиз уни таний оласизми?** Siz uni taniy olasizmi?
Are you sure?	**Ишончингиз комилми?** Ishonchingiz komilmi?

Please calm down.	**Илтимос, тинчланинг.** Iltimos, tinchlaning.
Take it easy!	**Ҳовлиқмасдан!** Hovliqmasdan!
Don't worry!	**Ташвишланманг.** Tashvishlanmang.
Everything will be fine.	**Ҳаммаси жойида бўлади.** Hammasi joyida bo'ladi.

Everything's all right.	**Ҳаммаси жойида.** Hammasi joyida.
Come here, please.	**Олдимга келинг, илтимос.** Oldimga keling, iltimos.
I have some questions for you.	**Сизга бир нечта саволим бор.** Sizga bir nechta savolim bor.
Wait a moment, please.	**Тўхтаб туринг, илтимос.** To'xtab turing, iltimos.
Do you have any I.D.?	**Ҳужжатларингиз борми?** Hujjatlaringiz bormi?
Thanks. You can leave now.	**Раҳмат. Боришингиз мумкин.** Rahmat. Borishingiz mumkin.
Hands behind your head!	**Қўлингизни бошингиз орқасига қилинг!** Qo'lingizni boshingiz orqasiga qiling!
You're under arrest!	**Сиз ҳибс этилдингиз!** Siz hibs etildingiz!

Health problems

Please help me.	**Илтимос, ёрдам беринг.**
	Iltimos, yordam bering.
I don't feel well.	**Аҳволим ёмон.**
	Ahvolim yomon.
My husband doesn't feel well.	**Эримнинг аҳволи ёмон.**
	Erimning ahvoli yomon.
My son …	**Ўғлимнинг …**
	O'g'limning …
My father …	**Отамнинг …**
	Otamning …
My wife doesn't feel well.	**Рафиқамнинг аҳволи ёмон.**
	Rafiqamning ahvoli yomon.
My daughter …	**Қизимнинг …**
	Qizimning …
My mother …	**Онамнинг …**
	Onamning …
I've got a …	**Менинг … оғрияпти.**
	Mening … og'riyapti.
headache	**бошим**
	boshim
sore throat	**томоғим**
	tomog'im
stomach ache	**қорним**
	qornim
toothache	**тишим**
	tishim
I feel dizzy.	**Бошим айланаяпти.**
	Boshim aylanayapti.
He has a fever.	**Унинг иситмаси бор.**
	Uning isitmasi bor.
She has a fever.	**Унинг иситмаси бор.**
	Uning isitmasi bor.
I can't breathe.	**Нафасим қисилаяпти.**
	Nafasim qisilayapti.
I'm short of breath.	**Нафасим бўғилаяпти.**
	Nafasim bo'g'ilayapti.
I am asthmatic.	**Мен астматик.**
	Men astmatik.
I am diabetic.	**Мен диабетик.**
	Men diabetik.

I can't sleep.	**Мени уйқусизлик қийнаяпти.** Meni uyqusizlik qiynayapti.
food poisoning	**овқатдан заҳарланиш** ovqatdan zaharlanish
It hurts here.	**Бу ерим оғрияпти.** Bu erim og'riyapti.
Help me!	**Ёрдам беринг!** Yordam bering!
I am here!	**Мен бу ерда!** Men bu erda!
We are here!	**Биз бу ерда!** Biz bu erda!
Get me out of here!	**Мени чиқариб олинг!** Meni chiqarib oling!
I need a doctor.	**Менга врач керак.** Menga vrach kerak.
I can't move.	**Мен қимирлай олмаяпман.** Men qimirlay olmayapman.
I can't move my legs.	**Оёқларимни сезмаяпман.** Oyoqlarimni sezmayapman.
I have a wound.	**Мен ярадорман.** Men yaradorman.
Is it serious?	**Бу жиддийми?** Bu jiddiymi?
My documents are in my pocket.	**Ҳужжатларим чўнтагимда.** Hujjatlarim cho'ntagimda.
Calm down!	**Тинчланинг!** Tinchlaning!
May I use your phone?	**Қўнғироқ қилсам бўладими?** Qo'ng'iroq qilsam bo'ladimi?
Call an ambulance!	**Тез ёрдам чақиринг!** Tez yordam chaqiring!
It's urgent!	**Бу зарур!** Bu zarur!
It's an emergency!	**Бу жуда зарур!** Bu juda zarur!
Please hurry up!	**Илтимос, тезроқ!** Iltimos, tezroq!
Would you please call a doctor?	**Врачни чақиртиринг, илтимос.** Vrachni chaqirtiring, iltimos.
Where is the hospital?	**Шифохонанинг қаердалигини айтиб юборинг?** Shifoxonaning qaerdaligini aytib yuboring?
How are you feeling?	**Ўзингизни қандай ҳис этаяпсиз?** O'zingizni qanday his etayapsiz?
Are you all right?	**Аҳволингиз яхшими?** Ahvolingiz yaxshimi?

What's happened?	**Нима бўлди?** Nima bo'ldi?
I feel better now.	**Аҳволим бироз дуруст.** Ahvolim biroz durust.
It's OK.	**Ҳаммаси жойида.** Hammasi joyida.
It's all right.	**Ҳаммаси яхши.** Hammasi yaxshi.

At the pharmacy

pharmacy (drugstore)
дорихона
dorixona

24-hour pharmacy
туну-кун ишлайдиган дорихона
tunu-kun ishlaydigan dorixona

Where is the closest pharmacy?
Энг яқин дорихона қаерда?
Eng yaqin dorixona qaerda?

Is it open now?
У ҳозир очиқми?
U hozir ochiqmi?

At what time does it open?
У нечада очилади?
U nechada ochiladi?

At what time does it close?
У соат нечагача ишлайди?
U soat nechagacha ishlaydi?

Is it far?
Бу узоқми?
Bu uzoqmi?

Can I get there on foot?
У ерга пиёда бора оламанми?
U erga piyoda bora olamanmi?

Can you show me on the map?
Илтимос, харитада кўрсатиб юборинг.
Iltimos, xaritada ko'rsatib yuboring.

Please give me something for …
Менга ... бирор нарса беринг.
Menga ... biror narsa bering.

a headache
бош оғриқдан
bosh og'riqdan

a cough
йўталдан
yo'taldan

a cold
шамоллашдан
shamollashdan

the flu
тумовдан
tumovdan

a fever
ҳароратдан
haroratdan

a stomach ache
ошқозон оғриғидан
oshqozon og'rig'idan

nausea
кўнгил айнишидан
ko'ngil aynishidan

diarrhea
ич оғриғидан
ich og'rig'idan

constipation
ич қотишидан
ich qotishidan

pain in the back	**бел оғриғидан** bel og'rig'idan
chest pain	**кўкрак оғриғидан** ko'krak og'rig'idan
side stitch	**биқин оғриғидан** biqin og'rig'idan
abdominal pain	**қорин оғриғидан** qorin og'rig'idan
pill	**таблетка** tabletka
ointment, cream	**малҳам, крем** malham, krem
syrup	**шарбат** sharbat
spray	**спрей** sprey
drops	**томчилар** tomchilar
You need to go to the hospital.	**Сиз шифохонага боришингиз керак.** Siz shifoxonaga borishingiz kerak.
health insurance	**кафолат** kafolat
prescription	**дори қоғоз** dori qog'oz
insect repellant	**ҳашаротга қарши восита** hasharotga qarshi vosita
Band Aid	**лейкопластир** leykoplastir

The bare minimum

Excuse me, ...	**Кечирасиз, ...** Kechirasiz, ...
Hello.	**Ассалому алайкум.** Assalomu alaykum.
Thank you.	**Рахмат.** Rahmat.
Good bye.	**Кўришгунча.** Ko'rishguncha.
Yes.	**Ха.** Ha.
No.	**Йўқ.** Yo'q.
I don't know.	**Билмайман.** Bilmayman.
Where? | Where to? | When?	**Қаерда? | Қаерга? | Қачон?** Qaerda? | Qaerga? | Qachon?

I need ...	**Менга ... керак.** Menga ... kerak.
I want ...	**Мен ... хохлайман.** Men ... xohlayman.
Do you have ...?	**Сизда ... борми?** Sizda ... bormi?
Is there a ... here?	**Бу ерда ... борми?** Bu erda ... bormi?
May I ...?	**Мен ... бўладими?** Men ... bo'ladimi?
..., please (polite request)	**Мархамат қилиб** Marhamat qilib

I'm looking for ...	**Мен ... қидираяпман.** Men ... qidirayapman.
the restroom	**хожатхона** hojatxona
an ATM	**банкомат** bankomat
a pharmacy (drugstore)	**дорихона** dorixona
a hospital	**шифохона** shifoxona
the police station	**милиция бўлимини** militsiya bo'limini
the subway	**метро** metro

a taxi	**такси** taksi
the train station	**вокзал** vokzal

My name is …	**Менинг исмим …** Mening ismim …
What's your name?	**Исмингиз нима?** Ismingiz nima?
Could you please help me?	**Менга ёрдам бериб юборинг, илтимос.** Menga yordam berib yuboring, iltimos.

I've got a problem.	**Менда бир муаммо бор.** Menda bir muammo bor.
I don't feel well.	**Аҳволим ёмон.** Ahvolim yomon.
Call an ambulance!	**Тез ёрдам чақиринг!** Tez yordam chaqiring!
May I make a call?	**Қўнғироқ қилсам бўладими?** Qo'ng'iroq qilsam bo'ladimi?

I'm sorry.	**Узр, …** Uzr, …
You're welcome.	**Арзимайди** Arzimaydi

I, me	**мен** men
you (inform.)	**сен** sen
he	**у** u
she	**у** u
they (masc.)	**улар** ular
they (fem.)	**улар** ular
we	**биз** biz
you (pl)	**сиз** siz
you (sg, form.)	**Сиз** Siz

ENTRANCE	**КИРИШ** KIRISH
EXIT	**ЧИҚИШ** CHIQISH
OUT OF ORDER	**ИШЛАМАЙДИ** ISHLAMAYDI

CLOSED	**ЁПИҚ**
	YOPIQ
OPEN	**ОЧИҚ**
	OCHIQ
FOR WOMEN	**АЁЛЛАР УЧУН**
	AYOLLAR UCHUN
FOR MEN	**ЭРКАКЛАР УЧУН**
	ERKAKLAR UCHUN

MINI DICTIONARY

This section contains 250
useful words required for
everyday communication.
You will find the names of
months and days of the week
here. The dictionary also
contains topics such as colors,
measurements, family, and
more

T&P Books Publishing

DICTIONARY CONTENTS

T&P Books Publishing

time	вақт	vaqt
hour	соат	soat
half an hour	ярим соат	yarim soat
minute	дақиқа	daqiqa
second	сония	soniya
today (adv)	бугун	bugun
tomorrow (adv)	ертага	ertaga
yesterday (adv)	кеча	kecha
Monday	душанба	dushanba
Tuesday	сешанба	seshanba
Wednesday	чоршанба	chorshanba
Thursday	пайшанба	payshanba
Friday	жума	juma
Saturday	шанба	shanba
Sunday	якшанба	yakshanba
day	кун	kun
working day	иш куни	ish kuni
public holiday	байрам куни	bayram kuni
weekend	дам олиш кунлари	dam olish kunlari
week	ҳафта	hafta
last week (adv)	ўтган ҳафта	o'tgan hafta
next week (adv)	келгуси ҳафтада	kelgusi haftada
in the morning	ерталаб	ertalab
in the afternoon	тушликдан сўнг	tushlikdan so'ng
in the evening	кечқурун	kechqurun
tonight (this evening)	бугун кечқурун	bugun kechqurun
at night	тунда	tunda
midnight	ярим тун	yarim tun
January	январ	yanvar
February	феврал	fevral
March	март	mart
April	апрел	aprel
May	май	may
June	июн	iyun
July	июл	iyul
August	август	avgust

September	сентябр	sentyabr
October	октябр	oktyabr
November	ноябр	noyabr
December	декабр	dekabr

in spring	баҳорда	bahorda
in summer	ёзда	yozda
in fall	кузгда	kuzgda
in winter	қишда	qishda

month	ой	oy
season (summer, etc.)	мавсум	mavsum
year	йил	yil

2. Numbers. Numerals

0 zero	нол	nol
1 one	бир	bir
2 two	икки	ikki
3 three	уч	uch
4 four	тўрт	to'rt

5 five	беш	besh
6 six	олти	olti
7 seven	етти	etti
8 eight	саккиз	sakkiz
9 nine	тўққиз	to'qqiz
10 ten	ўн	o'n

11 eleven	ўн бир	o'n bir
12 twelve	ўн икки	o'n ikki
13 thirteen	ўн уч	o'n uch
14 fourteen	ўн тўрт	o'n to'rt
15 fifteen	ўн беш	o'n besh

16 sixteen	ўн олти	o'n olti
17 seventeen	ўн етти	o'n etti
18 eighteen	ўн саккиз	o'n sakkiz
19 nineteen	ўн тўққиз	o'n to'qqiz

20 twenty	йигирма	yigirma
30 thirty	ўттиз	o'ttiz
40 forty	қирқ	qirq
50 fifty	еллик	ellik

60 sixty	олтмиш	oltmish
70 seventy	етмиш	etmish
80 eighty	саксон	sakson
90 ninety	тўқсон	to'qson
100 one hundred	юз	yuz

200 two hundred	икки юз	ikki yuz
300 three hundred	уч юз	uch yuz
400 four hundred	тўрт юз	to'rt yuz
500 five hundred	беш юз	besh yuz
600 six hundred	олти юз	olti yuz
700 seven hundred	етти юз	etti yuz
800 eight hundred	саккиз юз	sakkiz yuz
900 nine hundred	тўққиз юз	to'qqiz yuz
1000 one thousand	минг	ming
10000 ten thousand	ўн минг	o'n ming
one hundred thousand	юз минг	yuz ming
million	миллион	million
billion	миллиард	milliard

3. Humans. Family

man (adult male)	еркак	erkak
young man	ёш йигит	yosh yigit
woman	аёл	ayol
girl (young woman)	қиз	qiz
old man	чол	chol
old woman	кампир	kampir
mother	она	ona
father	ота	ota
son	ўғли	o'g'li
daughter	қиз	qiz
parents	ота-она	ota-ona
child	бола	bola
children	болалар	bolalar
stepmother	ўгай она	o'gay ona
stepfather	ўгай ота	o'gay ota
grandmother	буви	buvi
grandfather	бобо	bobo
grandson	невара	nevara
granddaughter	набира	nabira
grandchildren	неваралар	nevaralar
uncle	амаки	amaki
aunt	хола	xola
nephew	жиян	jiyan
niece	жиян	jiyan
wife	хотин	xotin
husband	ер	er

married (masc.)	уйланган	uylangan
married (fem.)	турмушга чиққан	turmushga chiqqan
widow	бева аёл	beva ayol
widower	бева еркак	beva erkak

| name (first name) | исм | ism |
| surname (last name) | фамилия | familiya |

relative	қариндош	qarindosh
friend (masc.)	дўст	do'st
friendship	дўстлик	do'stlik

partner	шерик	sherik
superior (n)	бошлиқ	boshliq
colleague	ҳамкасб	hamkasb
neighbors	қўшнилар	qo'shnilar

4. Human body

body	тана	tana
heart	юрак	yurak
blood	қон	qon
brain	мия	miya

bone	суяк	suyak
spine (backbone)	умуртқа	umurtqa
rib	қовурға	qovurg'a
lungs	ўпка	o'pka
skin	тери	teri

head	бош	bosh
face	юз	yuz
nose	бурун	burun
forehead	пешона	peshona
cheek	юз	yuz

mouth	оғиз	og'iz
tongue	тил	til
tooth	тиш	tish
lips	лаблар	lablar
chin	енгак	engak

ear	қулоқ	quloq
neck	бўйин	bo'yin
eye	кўз	ko'z
pupil	қорачиқ	qorachiq
eyebrow	қош	qosh
eyelash	киприк	kiprik
hair	сочлар	sochlar
hairstyle	турмак	turmak

mustache	мўйлов	mo'ylov
beard	соқол	soqol
to have (a beard, etc.)	қўйиш	qo'yish
bald (adj)	кал	kal

hand	панжа	panja
arm	қўл	qo'l
finger	бармоқ	barmoq
nail	тирноқ	tirnoq
palm	кафт	kaft

shoulder	елка	elka
leg	оёқ	oyoq
knee	тизза	tizza
heel	товон	tovon
back	орқа	orqa

5. Clothing. Personal accessories

clothes	кийим	kiyim
coat (overcoat)	палто	palto
fur coat	пўстин	po'stin
jacket (e.g., leather ~)	куртка	kurtka
raincoat (trenchcoat, etc.)	плашч	plashch

shirt (button shirt)	кўйлак	ko'ylak
pants	шим	shim
suit jacket	пиджак	pidjak
suit	костюм	kostyum

dress (frock)	аёллар кўйлаги	ayollar ko'ylagi
skirt	юбка	yubka
T-shirt	футболка	futbolka
bathrobe	халат	xalat
pajamas	пижама	pijama
workwear	жомакор	jomakor

underwear	ич кийим	ich kiyim
socks	пайпоқ	paypoq
bra	бюстгалтер	byustgalter
pantyhose	колготки	kolgotki
stockings (thigh highs)	пайпоқ	paypoq
bathing suit	купалник	kupalnik

hat	қалпоқ	qalpoq
footwear	пояфзал	poyafzal
boots (e.g., cowboy ~)	етик	etik
heel	пошна	poshna
shoestring	чизимча	chizimcha
shoe polish	пояфзал мойи	poyafzal moyi

gloves	қўлқоплар	qo'lqoplar
mittens	бошмалдоқли қўлқоплар	boshmaldoqli qo'lqoplar
scarf (muffler)	бўйинбоғ	bo'yinbog'
glasses (eyeglasses)	кўзойнак	ko'zoynak
umbrella	соябон	soyabon
tie (necktie)	галстук	galstuk
handkerchief	дастрўмол	dastro'mol
comb	тароқ	taroq
hairbrush	тароқ	taroq
buckle	камар тўқаси	kamar to'qasi
belt	камар	kamar
purse	сумкача	sumkacha

6. House. Apartment

apartment	хонадон	xonadon
room	хона	xona
bedroom	ётоқхона	yotoqxona
dining room	йемакхона	yemakxona
living room	меҳмонхона	mehmonxona
study (home office)	кабинет	kabinet
entry room	даҳлиз	dahliz
bathroom (room with a bath or shower)	ваннахона	vannaxona
half bath	ҳожатхона	hojatxona
vacuum cleaner	чангютгич	changyutgich
mop	швабра	shvabra
dust cloth	латта	latta
short broom	супурги	supurgi
dustpan	хокандоз	xokandoz
furniture	мебел	mebel
table	стол	stol
chair	стул	stul
armchair	кресло	kreslo
mirror	кўзгу	ko'zgu
carpet	гилам	gilam
fireplace	камин	kamin
drapes	дарпарда	darparda
table lamp	стол чироғи	stol chirog'i
chandelier	қандил	qandil
kitchen	ошхона	oshxona
gas stove (range)	газ плитаси	gaz plitasi

electric stove	**електр плитаси**	elektr plitasi
microwave oven	**микротўлқин печи**	mikroto'lqin pechi
refrigerator	**совутгич**	sovutgich
freezer	**музлатгич**	muzlatgich
dishwasher	**идиш-товоқ**	idish-tovoq
	ювиш машинаси	yuvish mashinasi
faucet	**жўмрак**	jo'mrak
meat grinder	**гўштқиймалагич**	go'shtqiymalagich
juicer	**шарбацuққич**	sharbatsiqqich
toaster	**тостер**	toster
mixer	**миксер**	mikser
coffee machine	**кофе қайнатадиган**	kofe qaynatadigan
	асбоб	asbob
kettle	**чойнак**	choynak
teapot	**чойнак**	choynak
TV set	**телевизор**	televizor
VCR (video recorder)	**видеомагнитофон**	videomagnitofon
iron (e.g., steam ~)	**дазмол**	dazmol
telephone	**телефон**	telefon

www.ingramcontent.com/pod-product-compliance
Lightning Source LLC
Chambersburg PA
CBHW070841050426
42452CB00011B/2372